The Gig Bag Book of
PRACTICAL
PENTATONICS
for all Guitarists

Packed with over 500 riffs and examples, this handy reference guide is a must for all guitarists. Includes sections on theory, solo construction, and more.

by Matt Scharfglass

Project editor: Ed Lozano
Interior design and layout: WR Music

Order No. AM 948805
US International Standard Book Number: 978-0-8256-1700-3
UK International Standard Book Number: 0.7119.7599.X

Music Sales America

DISTRIBUTED BY

HAL•LEONARD®
CORPORATION
7777 W. BLUEMOUND RD. P.O. BOX 13819 MILWAUKEE, WI 53213

This book is dedicated to Sandra Dubrov, for resisting the temptation to tell me to grow up and get a real job; and to Marty and Lois Scharfglass, for their constant encouragement and the use of their living room.

Table of Contents

Introduction

If you're a rock or blues musician, even if you know absolutely nothing about music theory, chances are you've heard some mention of the pentatonic scale. You may have read about it in a guitar magazine or heard a music instructor or fellow musician speak of it. You're probably even using it yourself without knowing it.

As its name states, a pentatonic scale is simply a scale that contains five notes. In the context of Western popular music, there are two types of pentatonic scales: minor and major.

You've heard the minor pentatonic scale used countless times in rock and blues music; AC/DC's Angus Young has made a career of using the same five notes in his solos since the mid-1970s without ever repeating himself. Legendary players such as Jimmy Page, Jimi Hendrix, Eric Clapton, Stevie Ray Vaughan, and Eddie Van Halen have made it their trademark as well.

You won't have to go far to hear the major pentatonic scale either, given its popularity among country artists such as Albert Lee, southern rockers such as Duane Allman and Dickey Betts, and rhythm and blues pioneers such as Curtis Mayfield.

The appeal of these scales, as well as the reason for their widespread use, is in their logic and simplicity. With that in mind... congratulations on a smart purchase! In these pages you'll find over 400 pentatonic licks, all of which can be used as inspiration for building your own solos.

But that's not all. You'll also learn the concepts that produced these licks, so that instead of being limited to what's in this book, you'll be able to come up with your own licks. You'll be pleasantly surprised at how simple these concepts actually are, and once you've mastered them, your solos will always sound inspired and fresh.

To help you maximize the time you spend with this book, here are a few things to keep in mind.

• With the exception of one section devoted to open-string licks, every lick in this book is in *close position,* meaning no open strings. This way you'll be able to easily transpose a lick from one key to another key without having to worry about open strings clashing. For example, take a look at the following lick, which is in A:

Now let's say you have a song in C that you think this lick would be perfect for. Since C is three half-steps up from A, and each fret on the guitar equals one half-step, you would simply start the lick three frets up the neck to play it in C.

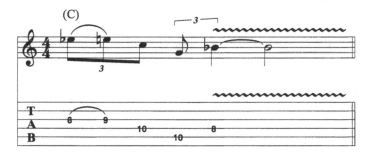

So if you see a lick you might want to use in one of your own solos, and the song you're playing happens to be in a different key, you now know how to change keys accordingly.

• *Don't think that in order to sound good, you have to play fast.* Licks, like the ones in this book, are the building blocks of a solo. Indeed, most of them will sound great when played at breakneck speeds, but what is far more important is your ability to play them in time, and *with feeling*. Speed-demon chops aren't just about talent; they're about stamina, coordination and technique, all of which are physical aspects of playing that anyone can train themselves to master. Just as with weight training, the more you repeat a motion, the easier it becomes to execute. If you practice, the chops will follow. So, take your time!

• *You're not limited to what's in this book.* Hey, you can even ignore the licks presented here if you want! The purpose of this volume is to help you understand pentatonic concepts; the licks are merely provided as a vehicle for you to apply these concepts to. If they serve as inspiration for your own solos, so much the better. In either case, seeing pentatonic principles used in a real-life context will help you learn them faster than by playing boring, clichéd exercises.

• On the other side of the coin, you may find that there are only portions of certain licks here that appeal to you. That's fine... there's no rule that says you have to learn every lick note-for-note in its entirety.

One final note: there's a lotta licks in this book. Though I've done my best to classify them, there's no way to alphabetize them for quick reference (unless you start giving them names like Herb or Sheldon). They are numbered; therefore, you may want to write down the numbers of those licks which really grab you as you play through this book.

Now the time has come for you to go forth, noble warrior... and bludgeon your adoring masses into submission with your pentatonic prowess. Enjoy!

Part 1: The Basics

Scales and Box Patterns

The beauty of the minor and major pentatonic scales is in their user-friendliness. Pentatonic scales fall into five very easy-to-play positions on the fretboard; these positions are commonly referred to as *boxes*. As you will see, the notes of the scales form a highly logical pattern within each box.

The Minor Pentatonic Scale

The A minor pentatonic scale is derived from the A natural minor scale, and is almost always used in rock and blues. The minor pentatonic scale contains the root (A), minor third (C), fourth (D), fifth (E), and minor seventh (G).

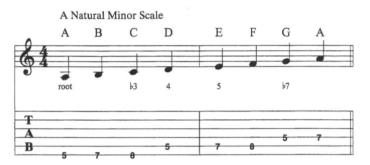

Each of the scale's five box patterns are shown graphically in a grid. The open circles on the grid indicate the root of the scale, which in this case is A. After you play through the scale associated with each box, go ahead and play the licks provided—just be sure you have the feel of the scale under your fingers first.

Box 1

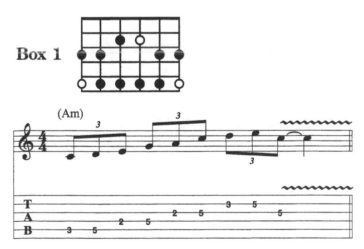

Told you it was easy, didn't I? Here are some box 1 licks.

1.

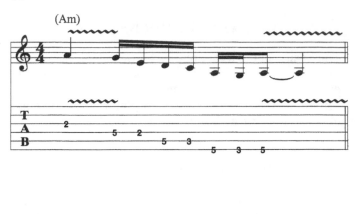

2.

This one's a very simple cascading line that descends and is easily executed without having to change your fret-hand position... thanks to the logic of box patterns. Use the pull-offs to help you gain speed.

3.

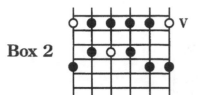

Box 2

Here are some box 2 licks.

4.

5.

6.

Box 3

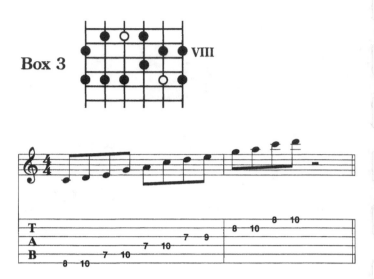

These funky licks fit very well into box 3.

7.

8.

9.

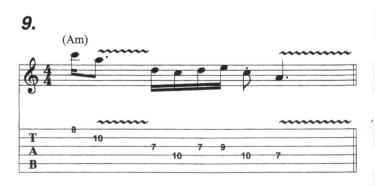

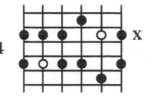

10.

11.

12.

Box 5

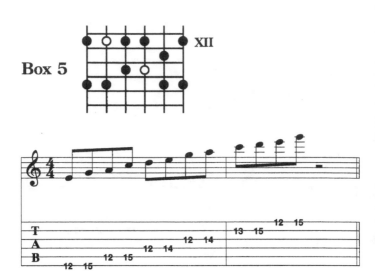

13.

14.

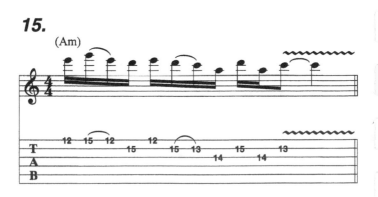

15.

The Major Pentatonic Scale

The major pentatonic scale is often found in country, old rhythm and blues, and southern-influenced rock. It is derived from the standard major scale, and contains the root (A), second (B), major third (C#), fifth (E), and sixth (F#).

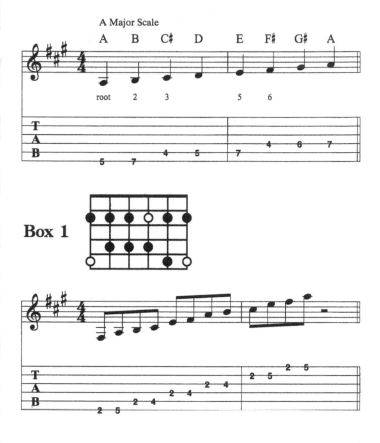

Box 1

This pair of licks has been used on many a bluegrass tune.

16.

17.

Here's another cascading box 1 pattern.

18.

Box 2

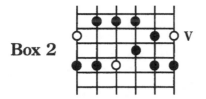

19.

20.

Box 3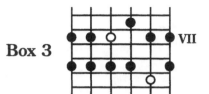

21.

Try this one over a slow funk groove.

22.

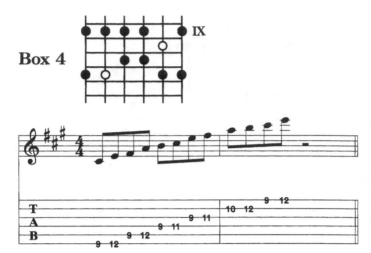

Box 4

23.

24.

Be sure to let the first two beats of this one ring out for a warm, down-home "a cappella" effect.

25.

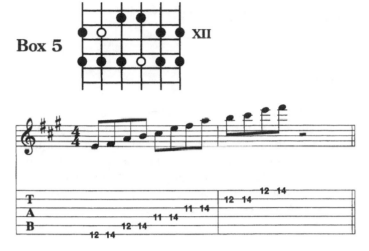

Box 5

I have only two things to say about this lick: (a) it covers the full range of notes offered by box 5, and (b) you might want to drink some water after playing it.

26.

Solo Construction

Slides

Now that you know how easy playing in box patterns is, here's the bad news: if you play in only one box, you'll be stuck with the range of notes that fall into that box only. This will result in your being limited to only a small number of licks. One way to remedy the problem is to simply slide from one box to another, which fortunately is a comfortable, natural-feeling task owing again to the logic of the fretboard.

The following lick effortlessly spans minor pentatonic boxes 1, 2, and 3 by using this technique.

27.

Also in minor pentatonic mode, this cascading, descending line spans boxes 5 and 4.

28.

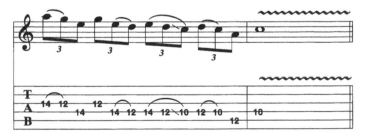

This popular minor sequence connects boxes 3, 2, and 1.

29.

As you can guess, box slides sit very comfortably in major pentatonic mode as well. Here's a country-flavored lick which spans boxes 3, 4, and 5.

30.

This chicken-pickin', ascending line spans boxes 2, 3, 4, and 5.

31.

Here's another descending sequence which begins in box 5 and ends seamlessly in box 2.

32.

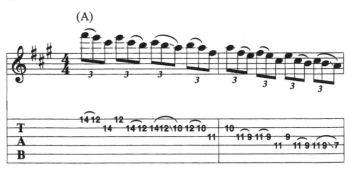

Adding Notes to the Pentatonic Scale

• **Minor pentatonic with flatted fifth.**

Another way to break out of the "box rut" is to simply add notes to the pentatonic scale. In minor pentatonic mode, the flatted fifth is, perhaps, the most frequently used note for this purpose because of the bluesy feeling it evokes. In fact, a minor pentatonic scale with an added flatted fifth is usually referred to as a *blues scale*.

Notice how easily the added flatted fifth falls into box 2.

33.

34.

• Minor pentatonic with major third.

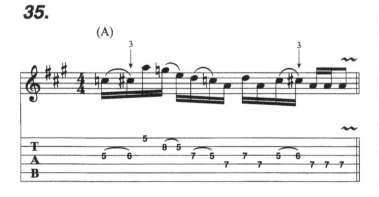

This combination is used very frequently in blues or blues-influenced rock. The tension between the minor third of the pentatonic scale and the added major third is what makes the minor pentatonic mode work so well even in major keys.

This scale degree also sits comfortably in box 2, as demonstrated by the following licks.

35.

36.

• Minor pentatonic with major sixth.

The major sixth gives a refreshing diminished sound to the minor pentatonic scale. Although it is often associated with jazz fusion, heavy rock guitarists such as Jimmy Page have put their stamp on it as well.

37.

Here is a variation on lick 37 showing both the added major sixth and the flatted fifth.

38.

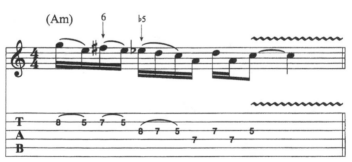

• Minor pentatonic with flatted sixth.

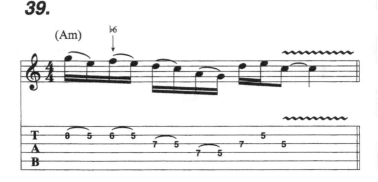

As shown in the previous scale, the added flatted sixth is a perfectly logical way to connect pentatonic scale degrees to each other, which allows for more fluid lines (a benefit for all you metal players).

39.

40.

• Minor pentatonic with second.

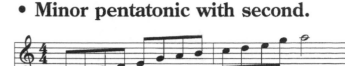

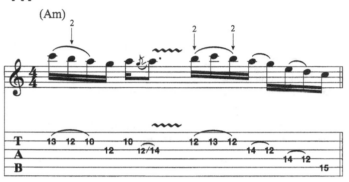

The added second is another logical way to connect pentatonic scale degrees.

41.

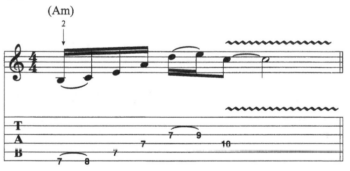

42.

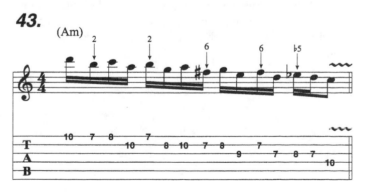

This cascading line features the minor pentatonic scale with the added flatted fifth, major sixth, and second, all neatly tucked away in box 3.

43.

Bends

It's been said that the guitar's timbre was intended to approximate the human voice. We already try to emulate human vocal qualities on the guitar by using vibrato; it should come as no surprise, then, that note-bending is probably an even more soulful and effective way to express emotion through a solo. It is a technique that allows the player to literally sing through his or her instrument, which is a great thing if you're like me and you can't carry a tune in a bucket.

Joy can be expressed with quick, light bends. Blues guitarists have been emoting sorrow with slow, almost wailing string bends since the 1930s. Rapid-fire pre-bends can be used to express aggression. The possibilities are limited only by the touch of the guitarist.

Bends are also great for another reason: they allow the guitarist to play many different notes without having to change frets or shift box positions, which is a great thing if you're like me and you're really lazy.

What does this have to do with pentatonics? The following lick falls into box 2 of the minor pentatonic scale. Notice how easy it is to hit the E note by bending the D on the seventh fret of the G string. Two notes for the price of one fret.

44.

Many guitarists bend notes higher than one whole step. As you play through this book you'll find that many of the licks contain bends up to two whole steps (with all points in between).

Up to this point we've covered what notes belong in a pentatonic lick. Now we'll cover how to make 'em sing by touching on some of the most commonly used types of bends.

• The quarter-tone bend.

When we sing, we sometimes miss notes by the slightest little bit. These hairline imperfections are what make us human, but they are also what people respond to, however unconsciously, when they hear a song they like. This quality can be emulated on the guitar quite effectively (and easily) by bending a note just a hair sharp; when done right, this subtle little trick can add a truckload of soulfulness to your sound.

As shown in the following example, a simple quarter-tone bend can take an ordinary pentatonic minor lick and turn it into a living thing.

45.

Notice how the quarter-tone bend at the end of this lick adds a sort of flirtatious quality to it.

46.

• The half-step bend.

Simply play a note and bend it up one half step.

47.

48.

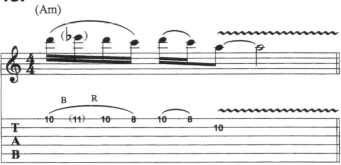

• The whole-step bend.

Bend the note up one whole step.

49.

50.

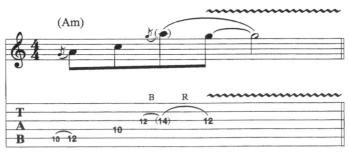

• The whole-step-and-a-half bend.

Bend the note up one and a half steps.

51.

52.

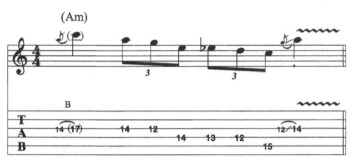

• The two-step bend.

Whole-step-and-a-half bend? Two-step bend? Geez, this is starting to sound either like an Olympic event or a square dance...

Anyway, as you can tell, the two-step bend simply means bend the note up two whole steps.

53.

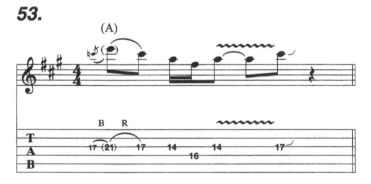

As mentioned earlier, many guitarists go even further, some bending notes as much as two and a half steps. It would go beyond the scope of this book to cover such a technique, not to mention that we don't want to be responsible for any injuries that may occur as a result...

• The pre-bend.

This involves bending a note up to a certain pitch before picking it, and then playing the already-bent note. As you can imagine, the pre-bend is probably the most difficult bend to execute because you won't know whether the bend is in tune or not until you play it!

The benefits of mastering pre-bends are obvious; besides just sounding great, they allow you to play licks that would otherwise be difficult to play using conventional fingerings.

54.

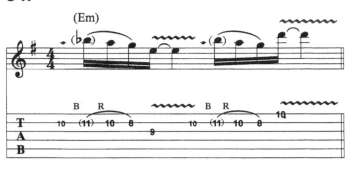

55.

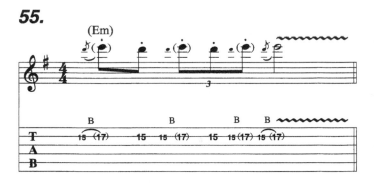

And, of course, pre-bends can be bent up to any interval you desire, from a quarter tone on up to whatever (as long as you don't break a string).

• The double-note bend.

This involves bending two notes at the same time. Usually, this is done on the G and B strings in the type of lick shown here.

56.

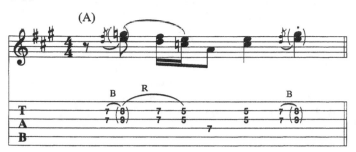

• The oblique bend.

The same as a double-note bend, except one note remains stationary while the other is bent.

57.

58.

• The unison bend.

I love this type of bend because it sounds so downright menacing with the right amount of volume. Unison bends are similar to oblique bends; one note is held down while another note, one whole step lower (on an adjacent string), is bent up to match the pitch of the stationary note. This type of bend is only executed on the B and high E strings together, or the G and B strings together.

59.

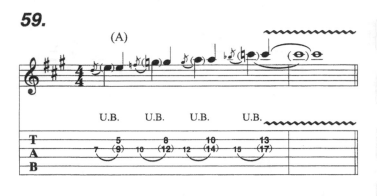

60.

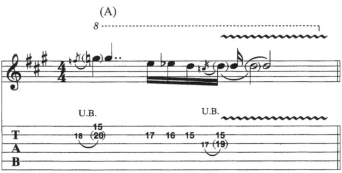

The key to effective note-bending, besides making sure your bends are in tune, is to remember that bends are about emotion. Even if you play metal, dig in! This is what set apart flashy players such as K. K. Downing (of Judas Priest) and the late Randy Rhoads from so many other guitarists that were prominent during the "speed" era of the early 1980s——a point certainly not lost on modern players such as Pantera's Dimebag Darrell and Alice In Chains' Jerry Cantrell.

Part 2: Library of Licks

Using Pentatonic Licks in a Careful, Responsible Fashion(!)

In the context of rock or blues music, one of the great many things about pentatonics is the way they can be used over virtually any standard chord progression.

As you become familiar with the licks in this book, you'll find that they work very well over many different chords. For instance, almost any minor pentatonic lick will sound good against an entire blues progression—not just the chord over which the lick is based. This means that an A minor pentatonic lick played over a D or E chord will sound just fine... you don't necessarily have to transpose a lick to E in order to play it over an E chord.

This rule doesn't apply only to blues; plenty of standard rock progressions complement pentatonic licks as well. Using the key of A again as an example, try playing any A minor pentatonic lick over the following chord progression:

$\frac{4}{4}$ C / / / | D / / / | A / / / | A / / / |

This works because the notes comprising the A minor pentatonic scale (A, C, D, E, and G) all coincide with (or complement) each chord in the progression that you just played.

Here's another fairly standard rock progression. Because it's in E minor, you'll want to try playing E minor pentatonic licks over it.

$\frac{4}{4}$ Em / / / | C / / / | G / / / | D / / / |

Again, the notes of the E minor pentatonic scale (E, G, A, B, and D) all occur naturally in this chord progression, so any E minor pentatonic lick is "safe."

The same principle works for blues. A blues progression in the key of A usually contains three chords: A, D and E. Once again, the notes of the A minor pentatonic scale coincide with each chord in the blues progression, meaning chances are fairly slim that a note from your solo will clash against the rhythm parts. Imagine not having to worry about playing the "right" notes!

In a nutshell: *just because a lick falls within a certain chord, it doesn't necessarily mean that you're stuck playing that lick over that chord only.*

Keeping this in mind will help you apply a newly-learned lick to a real-life situation where chords are constantly changing.

Lick Categories

Instead of lumping hundreds of licks into a big ol' pile and wishing you luck, I thought it might be easier (and more productive) to group some of the licks into broad categories for the sake of explaining what makes them different from others, and to perhaps draw your attention to certain techniques. The licks are not arranged in order of difficulty, so please feel free to skip around as desired. If you happen to play one that really jumps out at you, remember to write down the number for quick reference.

"Feel" Licks

I call the licks in this section "feel" licks because, though they look relatively simple, how good they sound depends on how much feeling, attitude, and conviction the player puts into them. Pay close attention to articulations such as staccato, vibrato and note-bending, and you'll soon have your guitar "singing" without having to shred a note! Here's an easy but tasty one to start with.

61.

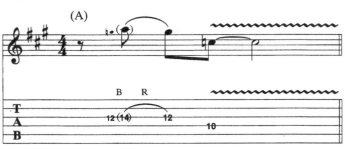

This one contains a nice, slow one-and-a-half-step bend. Be sure to keep the bend in tune when you execute the vibrato.

62.

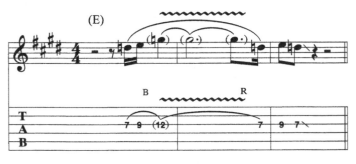

Here's a short, sweet, to-the-point way to start a solo.

63.

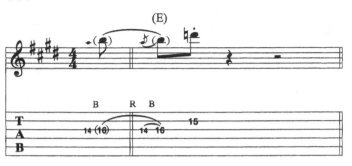

The rhythm on this one is a bit tricky, so you may want to count this one in 16 (four counts per beat) if you run into trouble.

64.

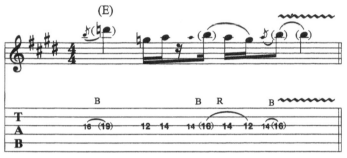

Be sure to really dig into the bends on these next few.

65.

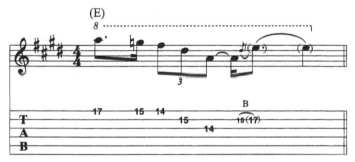

66.

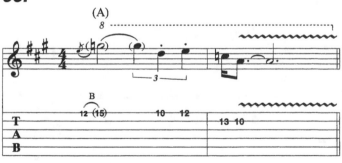

67.

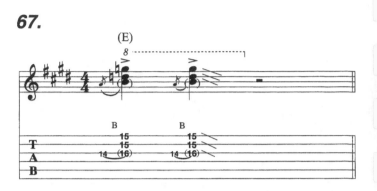

Though this one looks painfully simple, try playing it over an E minor chord. (Delicious, isn't it?)

68.

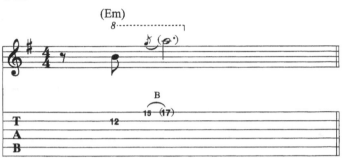

Now try connecting it to this lick.

69.

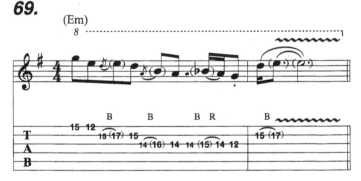

Some more bending licks to dig into...

70.

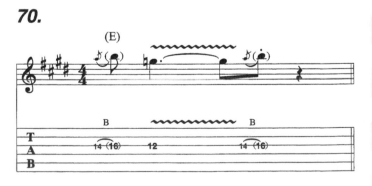

71.

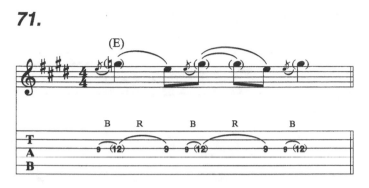

72.

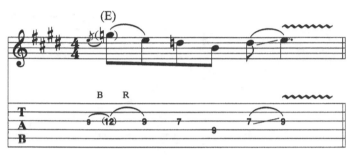

When played correctly, this one has an almost mournful quality to it.

73.

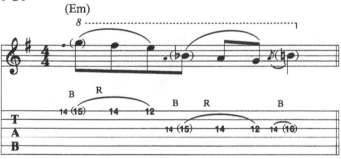

These licks pack a lot of attitude into a few notes.

74.

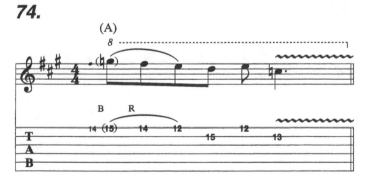

75.

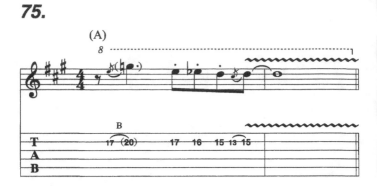

76.

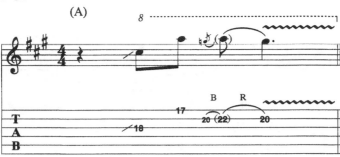

77.

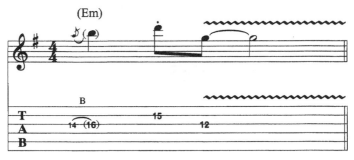

78.

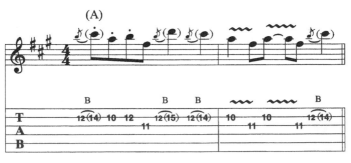

This one's a personal favorite because besides being easy to play, the triplet figure on the second beat just *oozes* attitude.

79.

The next three licks are very simple but effective ways to make a statement, with an ever-so-slight bend on the last note for emphasis.

80.

81.

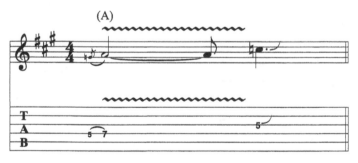

82.

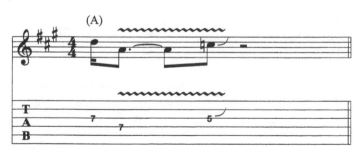

Dig in!

83.

84.

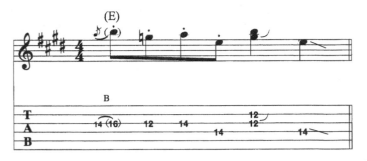

85.

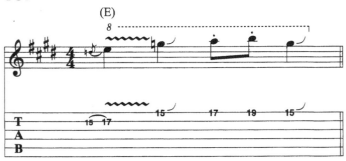

86.

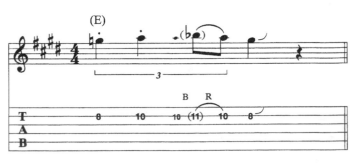

87.

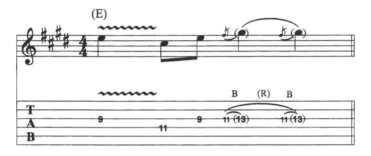

88.

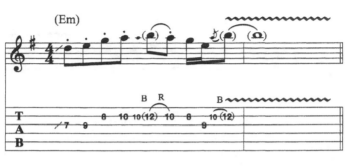

89.

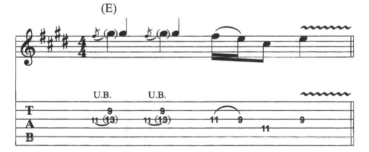

90.

91.

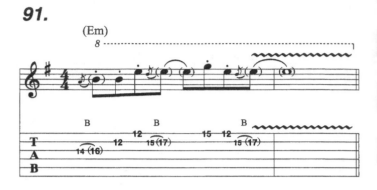

92.

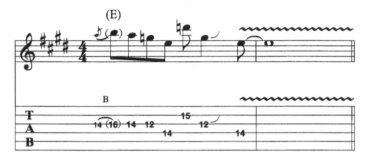

Unison bends are used here to build up to a climax.

93.

Repeating Licks

If you're Eddie Van Halen in the privacy of your practice space (like I am), and you become a sausage-fingered scaredy-cat on stage (like I am), repeating licks will save you. They're (a) easy to play, (b) time-honored by the likes of countless rock guitarists, (c) climactic, and (d) instantly recognizable by audiences everywhere, giving you automatic guitar-hero credibility whenever you pull one of these out of your bag of tricks. Try using one or two of these licks if you get stuck for an idea in the middle of a solo, and watch the excitement of your audience build (while you hopefully come up with a way to end your solo!).

94.

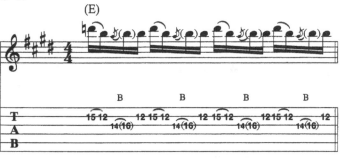

95.

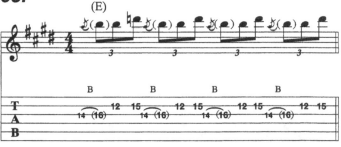

96.

Lick 97 is a slightly trickier variation on lick 96.

97.

98.

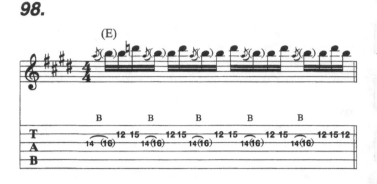

99.

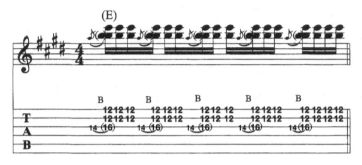

100.

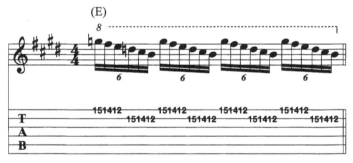

101.

Notice the displaced rhythmic feel of licks 102 and 103.

102.

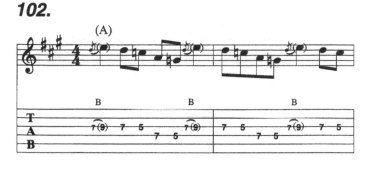

103.

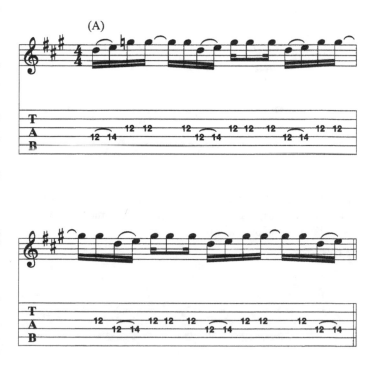

104.

105.

106.

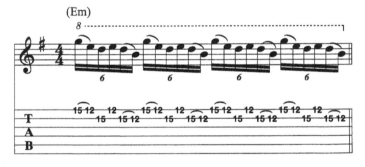

Licks 107 and 108 are great because they sound a lot more difficult than they actually are. They conveniently come in two flavors: major and minor.

107.

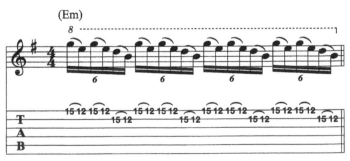

108.

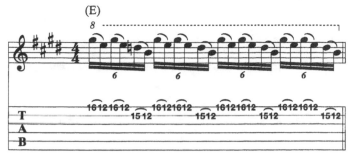

109.

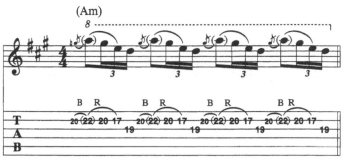

110.

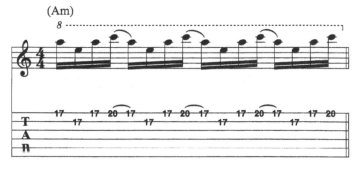

111.

112.

113.

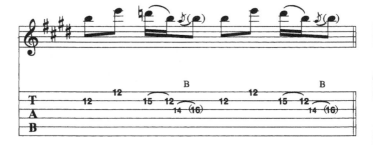

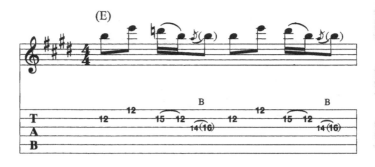

Note the bends (two whole steps) on this callus-builder.

114.

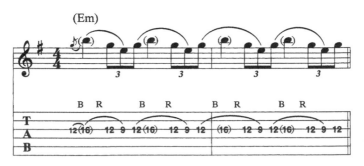

115.

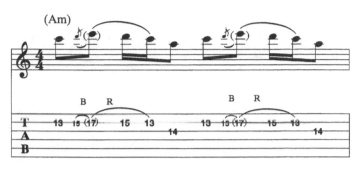

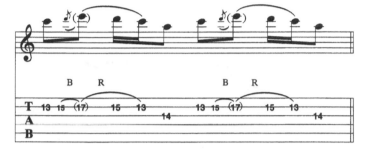

116.

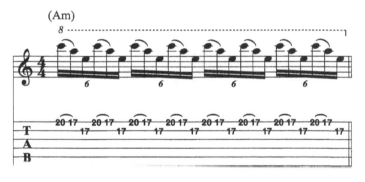

117.

118.

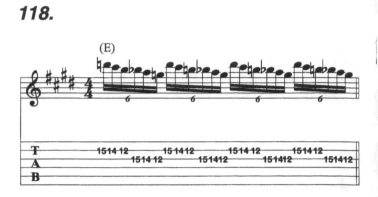

119.

Open-String Licks

This book wouldn't be complete if I didn't include a few licks involving open strings. Although they are a bit limiting because they can only be used in certain keys, they nonetheless sound great and can add flash to a solo with relatively little effort. Combined with the repeating lick concept covered in the last section, these are also quite effective for turning heads in the audience.

This one works wonderfully in A.

120.

Here's one in G that sounds cool because of the repeated notes in the middle of each sextuplet.

121.

The same fretting pattern can also be applied to the D, A, and E strings, meaning you can play the same lick in the keys of D...

122.

...or A.

123.

Following the same principle, here's another open repeating lick in the keys of E, A, D, and G.

124.

125.

126.

127.

Here are a couple of shredders in the key of E minor.

128.

129.

Also in E minor, this one packs a punch.

130.

Here's another open string pull-off lick which works in both A minor and E minor.

131.

132.

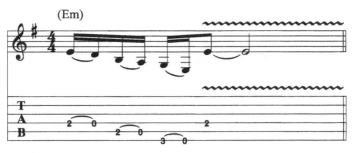

Last but not least, a couple of variations on a familiar E minor lick.

133.

134.

Double-Stop Licks

Made famous in popular music by players such as Jimi Hendrix and Curtis Mayfield, double-stops are a soulful way to add texture to a solo. Emphasis should be placed on digging in and making each note count when playing this type of lick.

These licks utilize the major pentatonic mode.

135.

136.

137.

This double-stop lick involves open strings.

138.

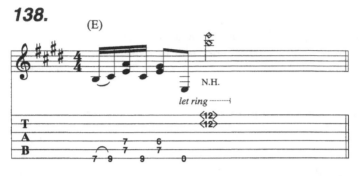

139.

Got the blues?

140.

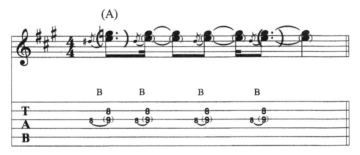

141.

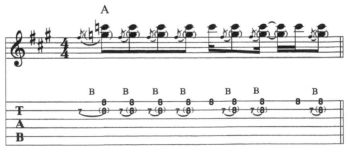

142.

The following are very effective in minor keys.

143.

144.

145.

Four licks for the price of one!

146.

147.

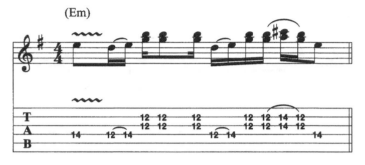

148.

149.

Here are some familiar faces.

150.

151.

152.

153.

Tricky Licks

None of the licks in this section are actually difficult, but they do contain subtle nuances to which you may want to pay special attention. Familiarity with the techniques used here will undoubtedly set you apart from many other players simply by the fact that these highly tasteful techniques aren't used very often.

The following licks utilize *partial releases,* which simply means bending a note up to a certain pitch and then releasing it slightly. For example, you would bend an F up one whole step to G, then release it only partially to an F sharp. The trick, obviously, is to keep the partially released note in tune.

154.

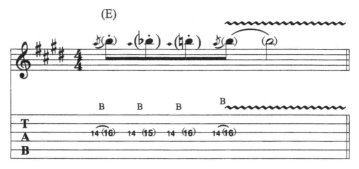

155.

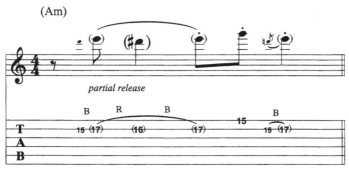

156.

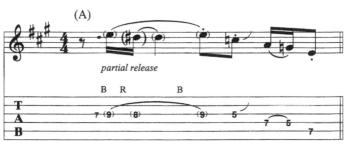

Here's a slight variation of this technique; notice how only the first note of the bend is picked.

157.

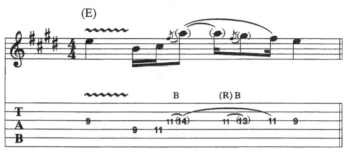

These four licks utilize bends executed with the index finger. You're probably accustomed to bending with your ring or pinky fingers; think of the musical possibilities that can open up by having one more finger to bend with.

158.

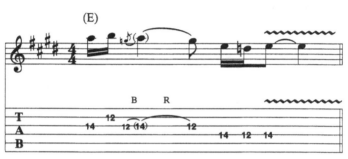

159.

160.

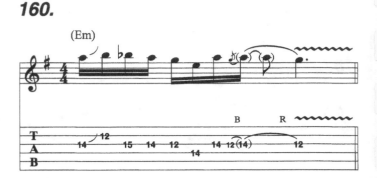

161.

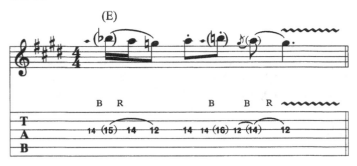

Here are a couple of tasty licks combining partial releases and index-finger bends.

162.

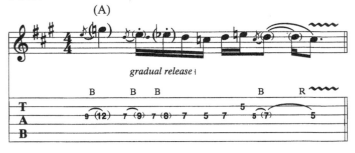

163.

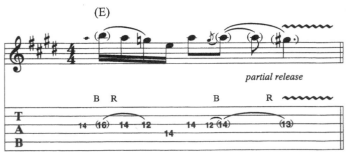

Finally, here's a group of licks that I consider to be somewhat tricky because of timing, rapid pre-bends, wide bends, and gradual releases.

164.

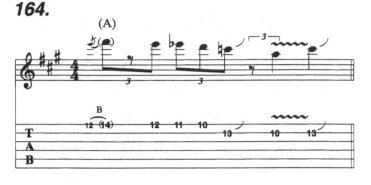

165.

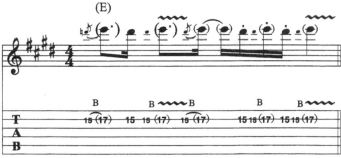

166.

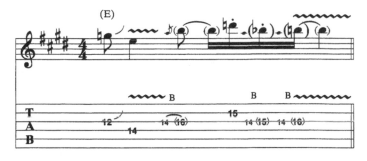

167.

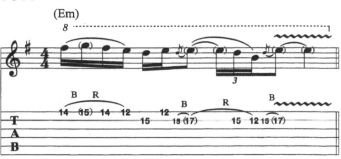

168.

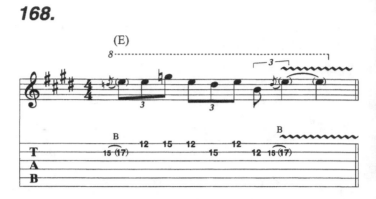

169.

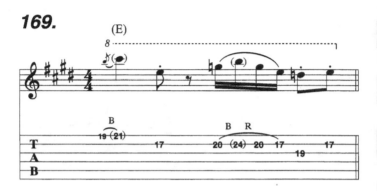

The Standards

The remainder of this book will be devoted to time-honored licks that have been used by all the greats. They can be mixed and matched any old way you like, and may even inspire you to come up with a few licks of your own. Go nuts...

170.

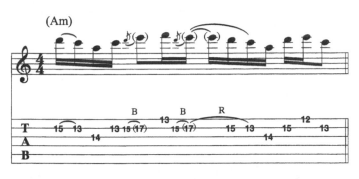

171.

172.

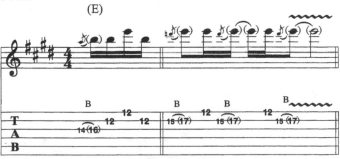

173.

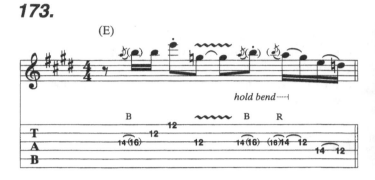

174.

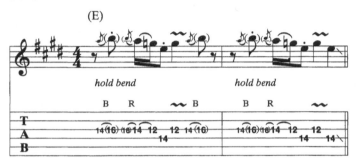

175.

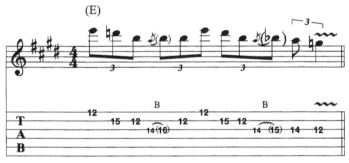

176.

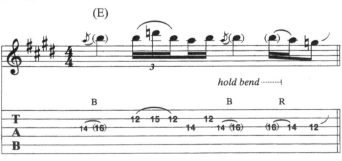

177.

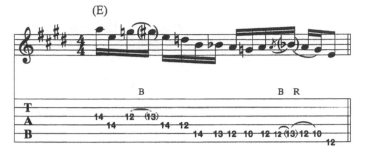

178.

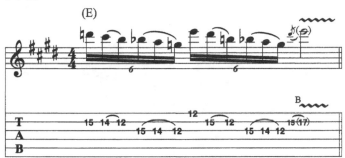

179.

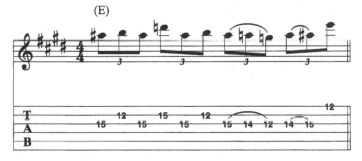

180.

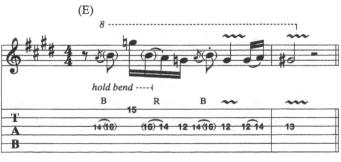

181.

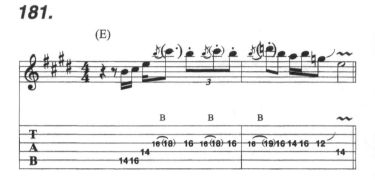

182.

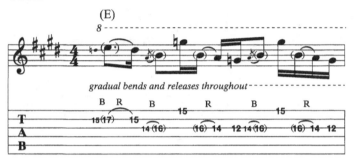

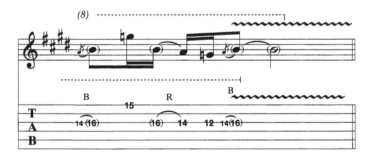

183.

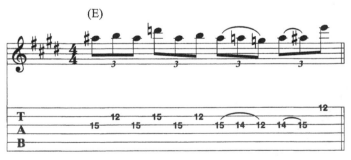

184.

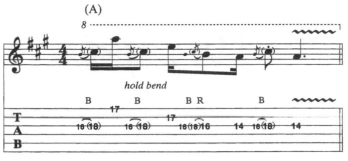

185.

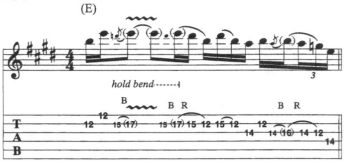

186.

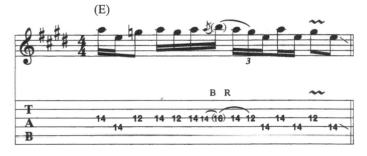

187.

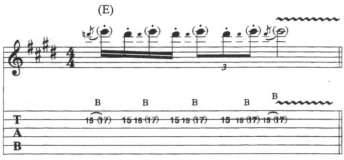

188.

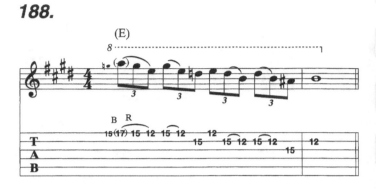

189.

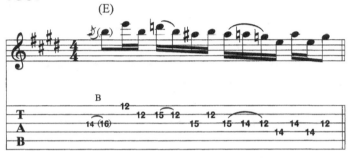

190.

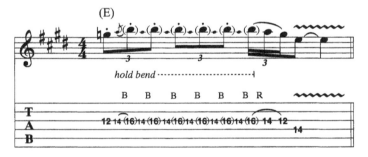

191.

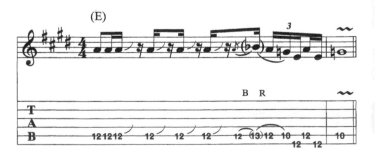

192.

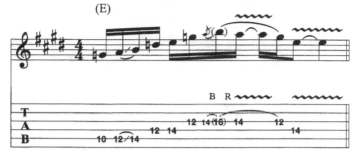

193.

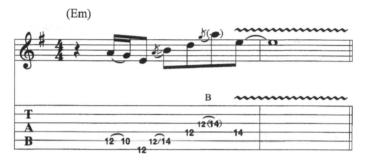

194.

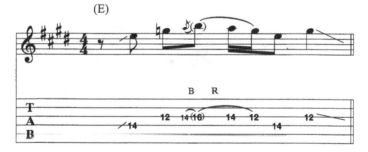

195.

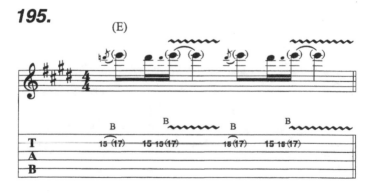

196.

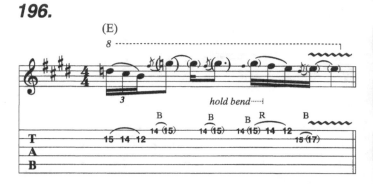

197.

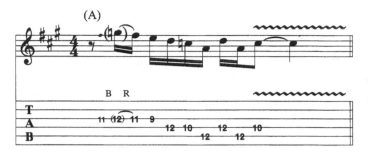

198.

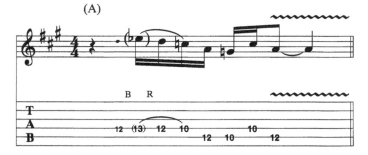

199.

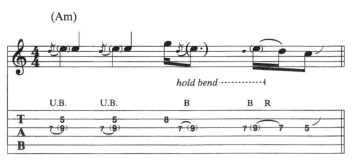

200.

201.

202.

203.

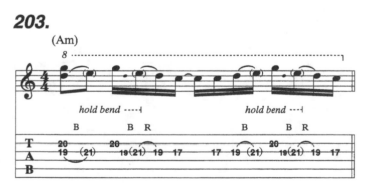

204.

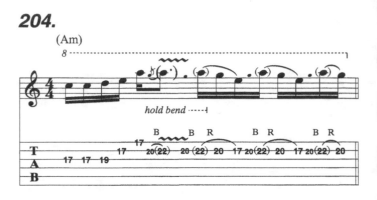

205.

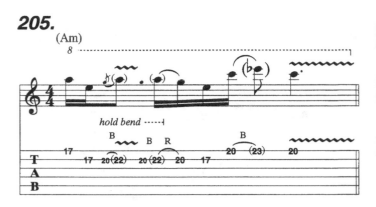

206.

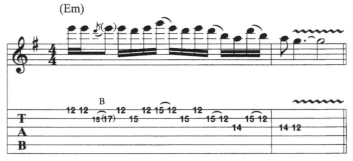

207.

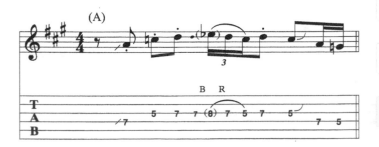

208.

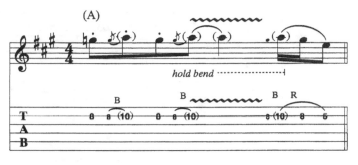

209.

210.

211.

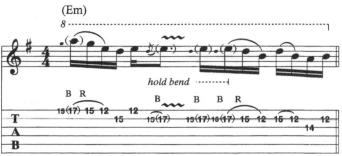

212.

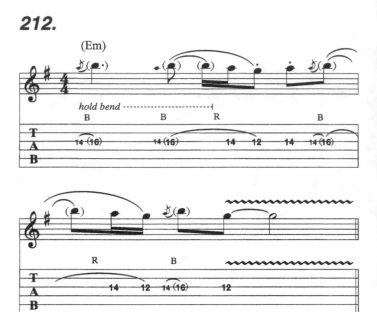

213.

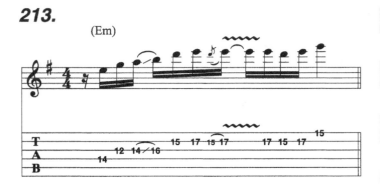

214.

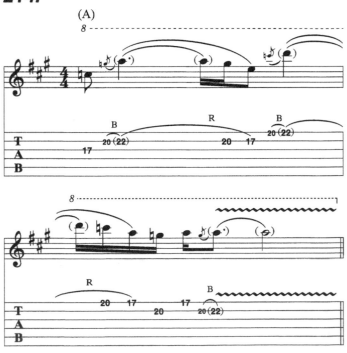

215.

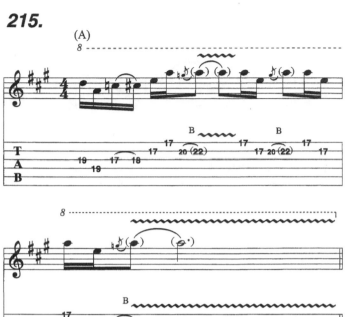

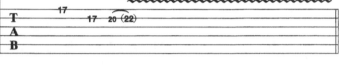

216.

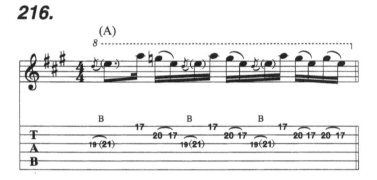

217.

218.

219.

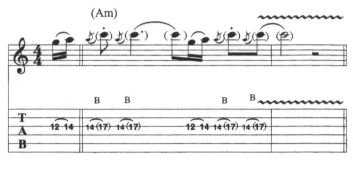

220.

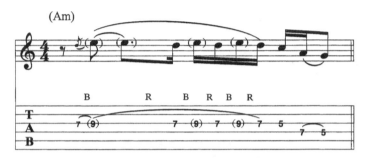

221.

222.

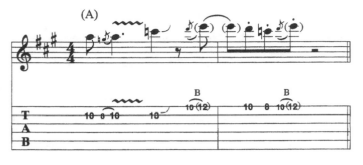

223.

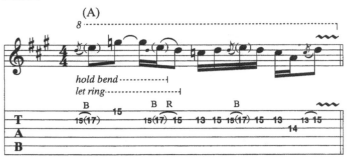

224.

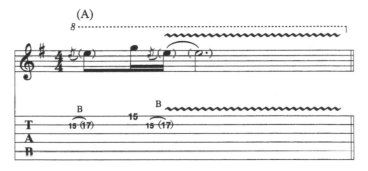

225.

226.

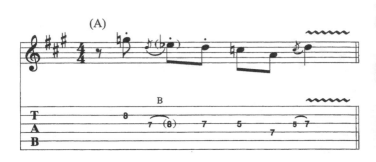

227.

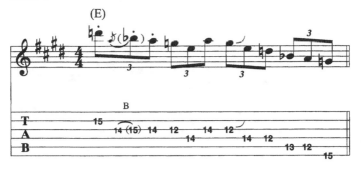

228.

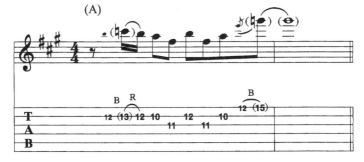

229.

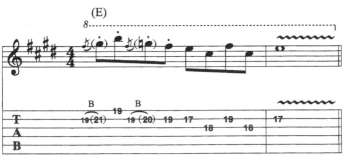

230.

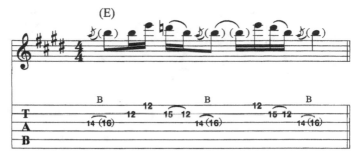

231.

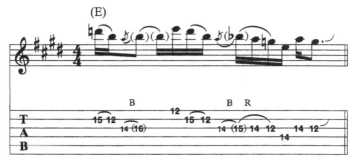

232.

233.

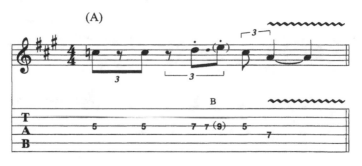

234.

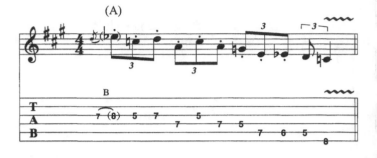

235.

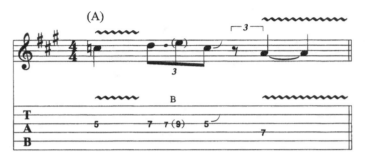

236.

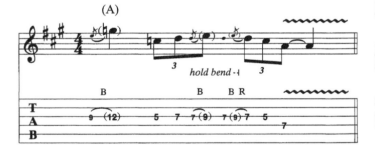

237.

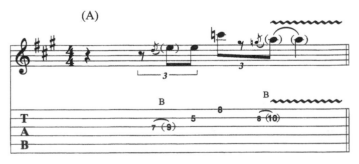

238.

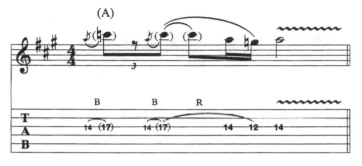

239.

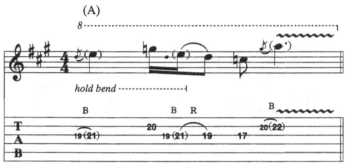

240.

241.

242.

243.

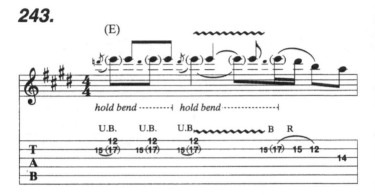

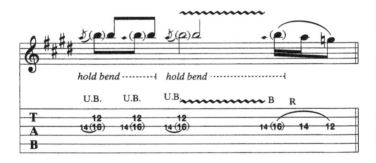

244.

245.

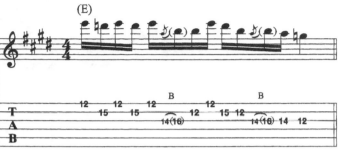

246.

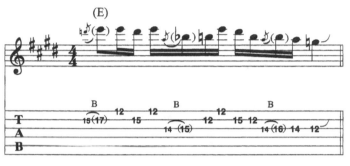

247.

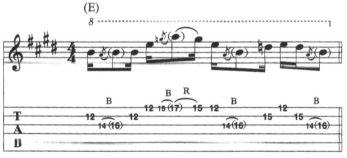

248.

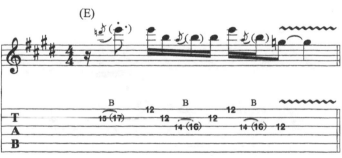

249.

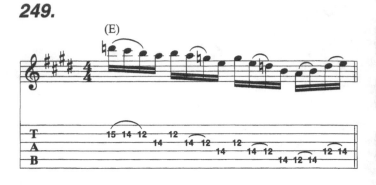

250.

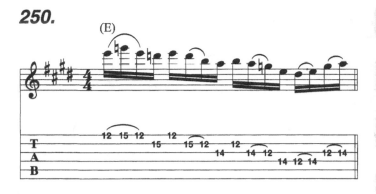

251.

252.

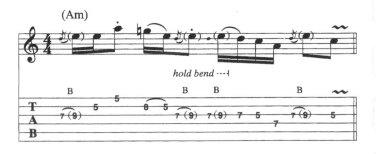

253.

254.

255.

256.

257.

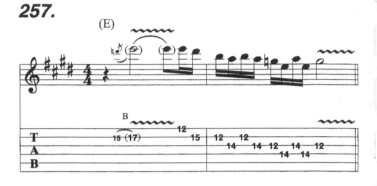

258.

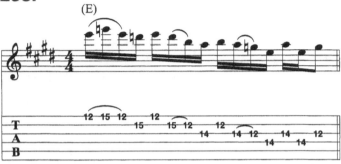

259.

260.

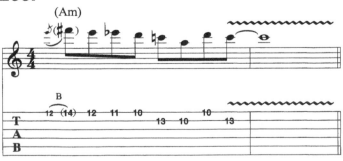

261.

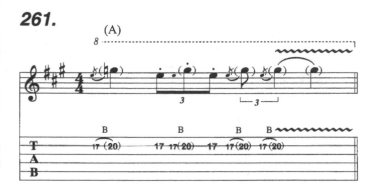

262.

263.

264.

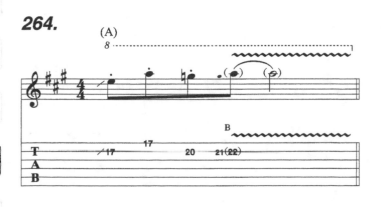

265.

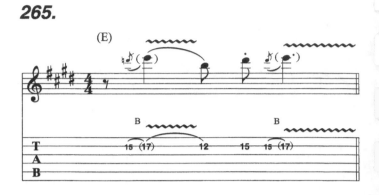

266.

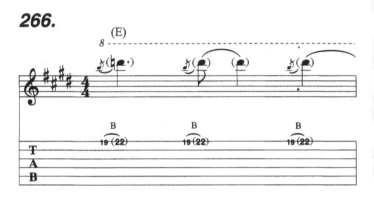

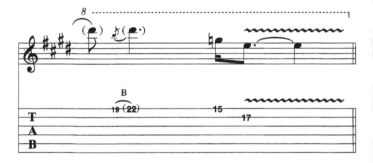

267.

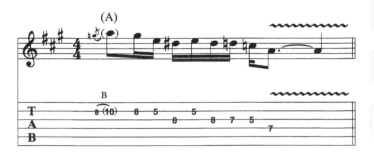

268.

269.

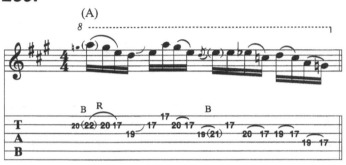

270.

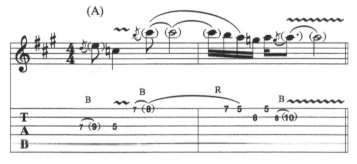

271.

272.

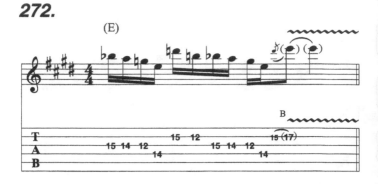

273.

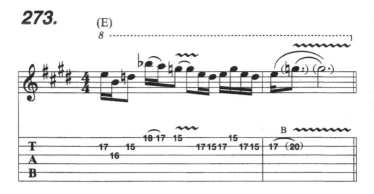

274.

275.

276.

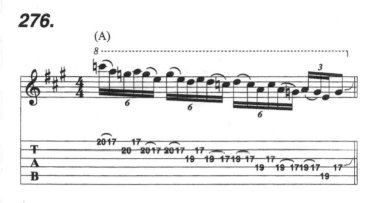

277.

278.

279.

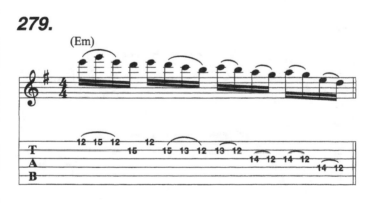

280.

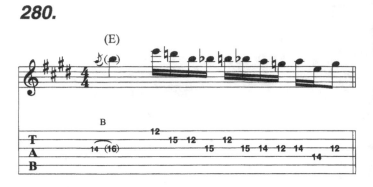

281.

282.

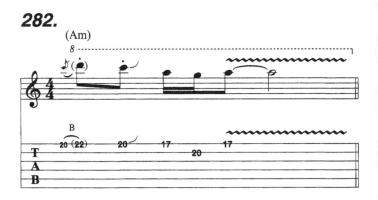

283.

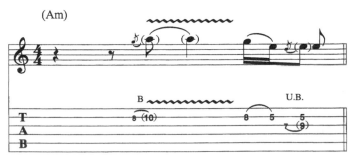

284.

285.

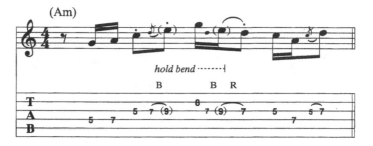

286.

287.

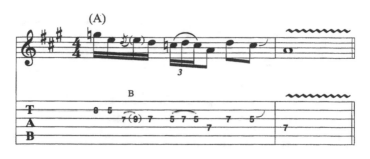

288.

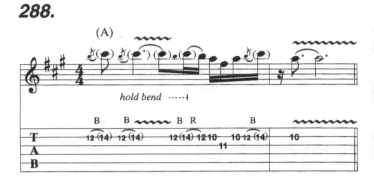

289.

290.

291.

292.

293.

294.

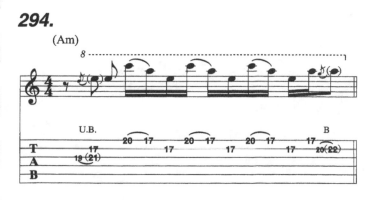

295.

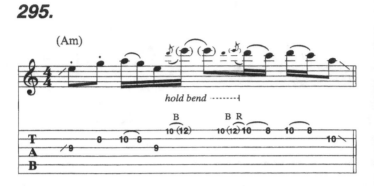

296.

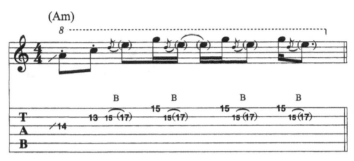

297.

298.

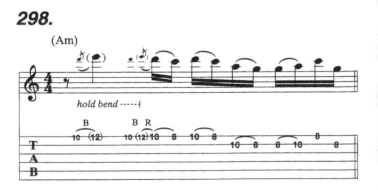

299.

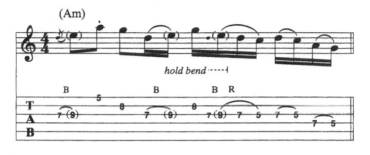

300.

301.

302.

303.

304.

305.

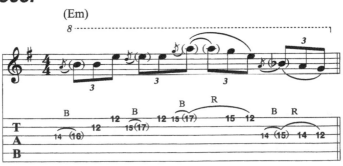

306.

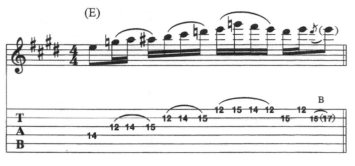

307.

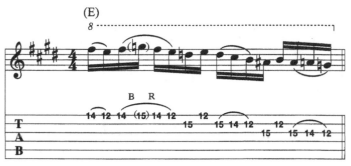

308.

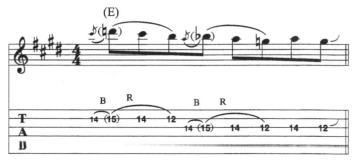

309.

310.

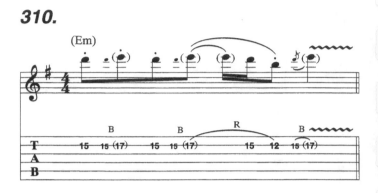

311.

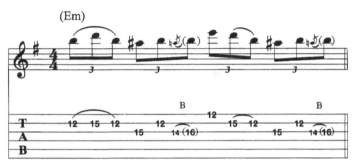

312.

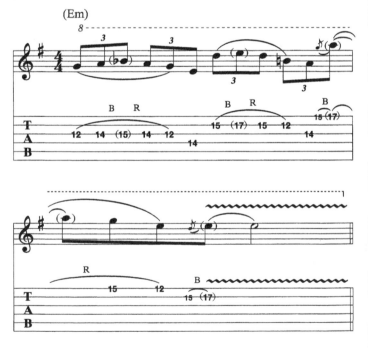

313.

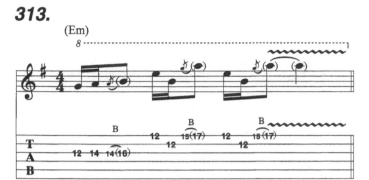

314.

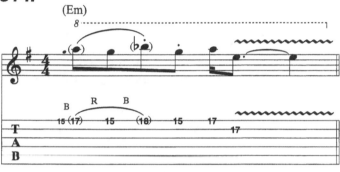

315.

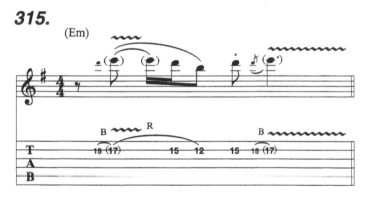

316.

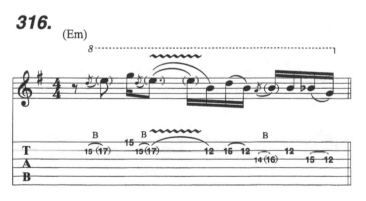

317.

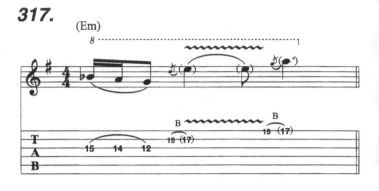

318.

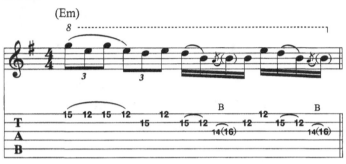

319.

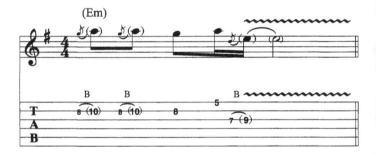

320.

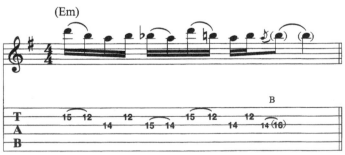

321.

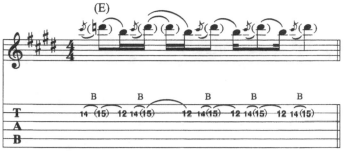

322.

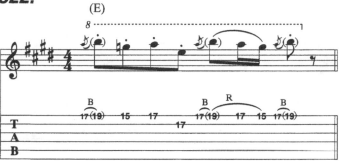

323.

324.

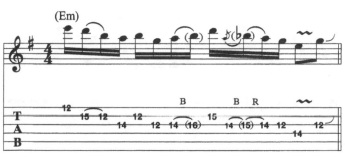

325.

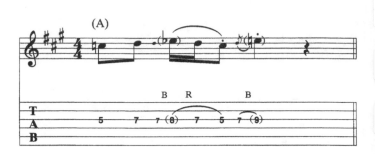

326.

327.

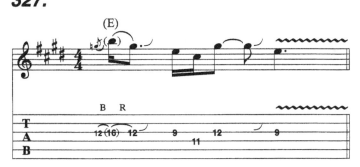

328.

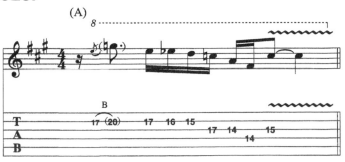

329.

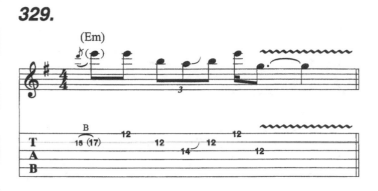

330.

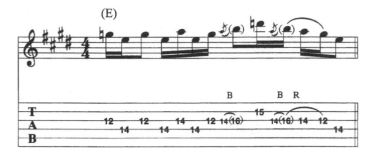

331.

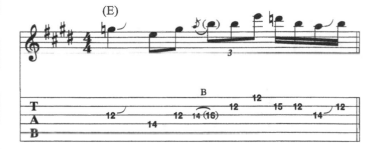

332.

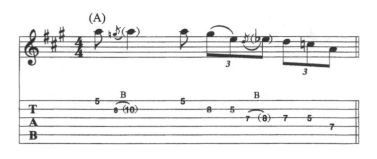

333.

334.

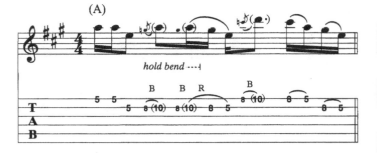

335.

336.

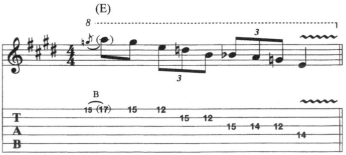

337.

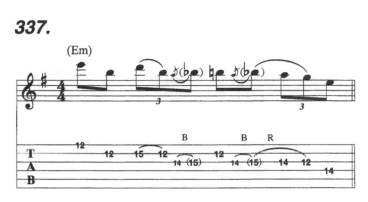

338.

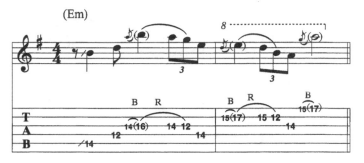

339.

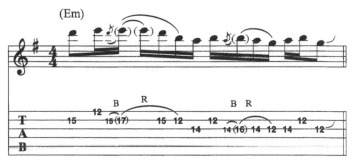

340.

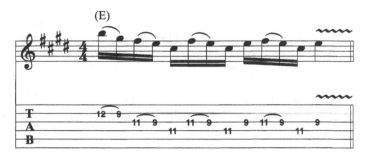

341.

342.

343.

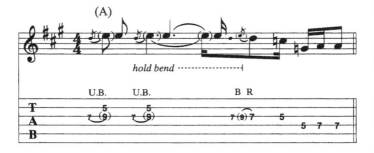

344.

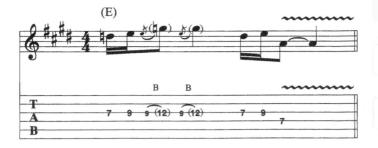

345.

346.

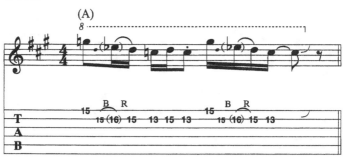

347.

348.

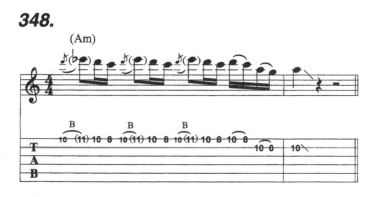

349.

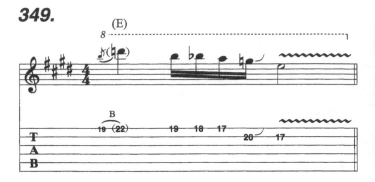

350.

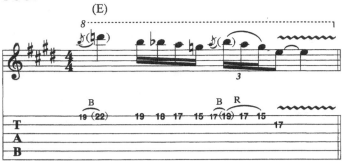

351.

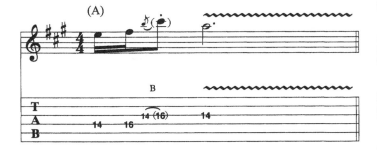

352.

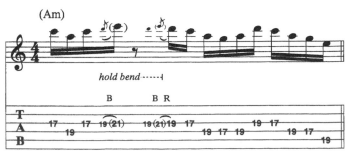

353.

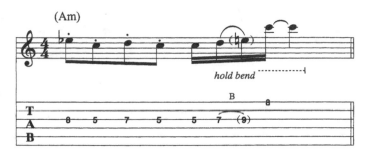

354.

355.

356.

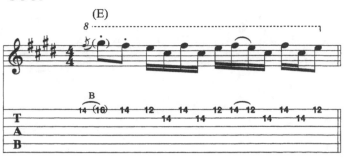

357.

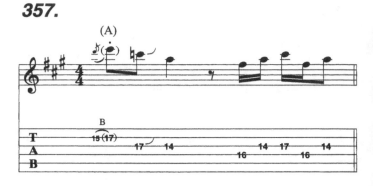

358.

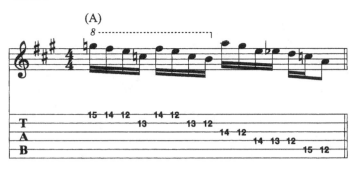

359.

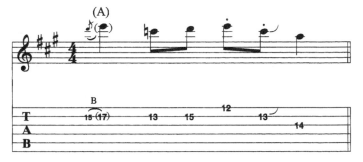

360.

361.

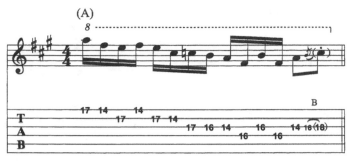

362.

363.

364.

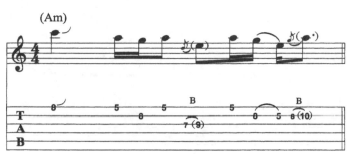

365.

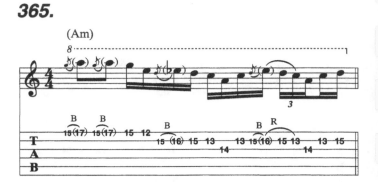

366.

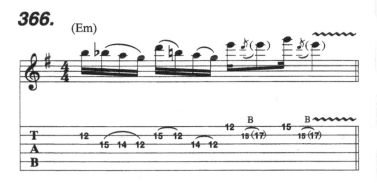

367.

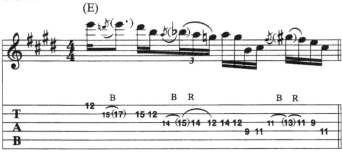

368.

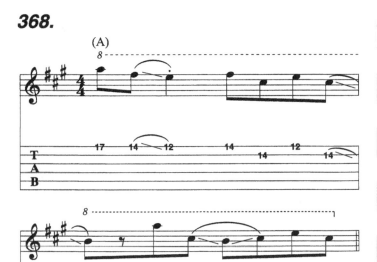

369.

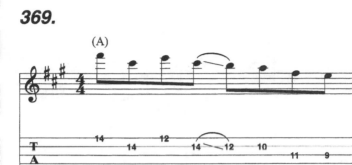

370.

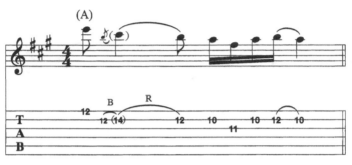

371.

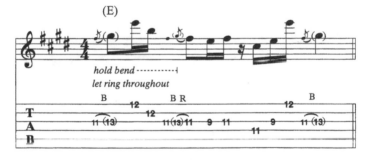

372.

373.

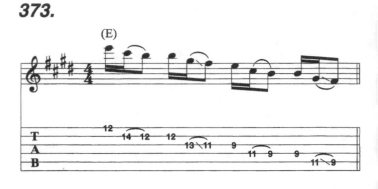

374.

375.

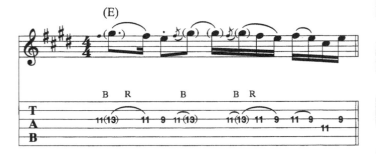

376.

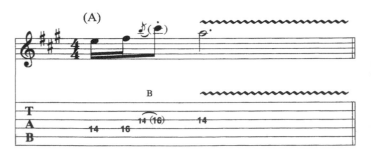

377.

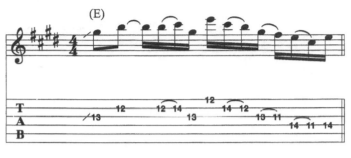

378.

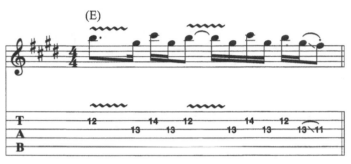

379.

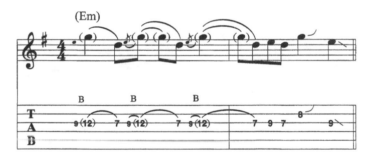

380.

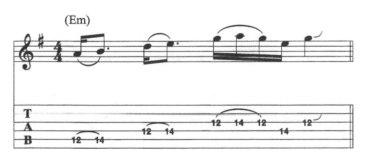

381.

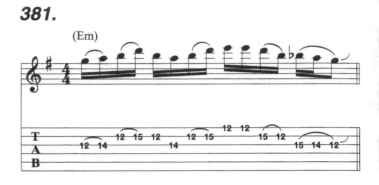

382.

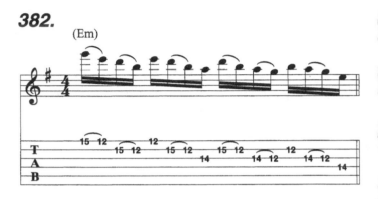

383.

384.

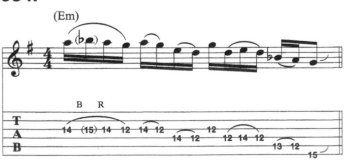

385.

386.

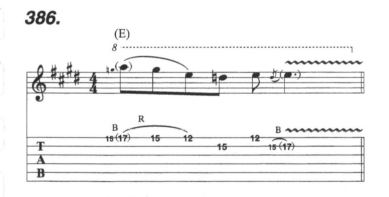

387.

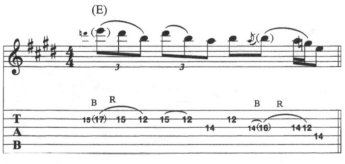

388.

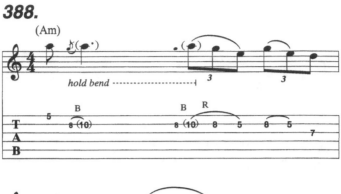

389.

390.

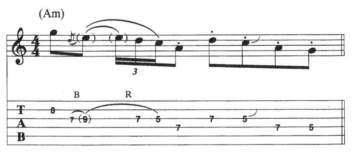

391.

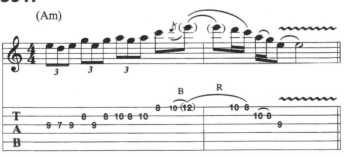

392.

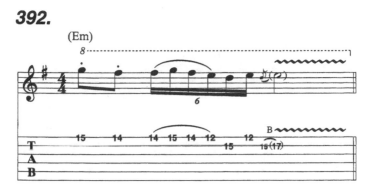

393.

394.

395.

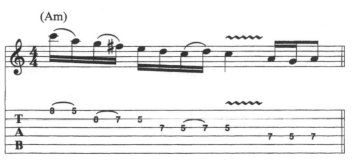

396.

397.

398.

399.

400.

401.

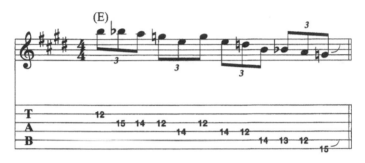

402.

403.

404.

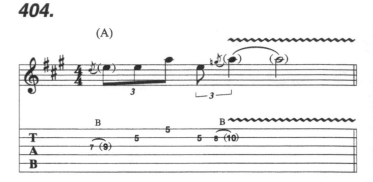

405.

406.

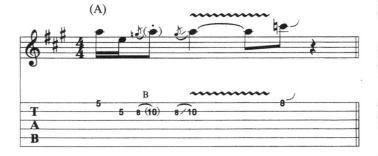

407.

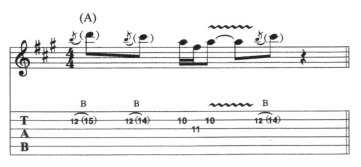

408.

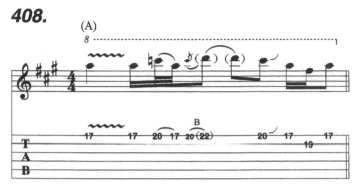

409.

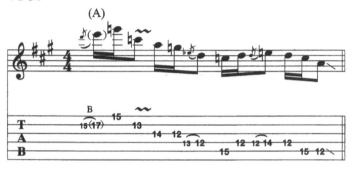

410.

411.

412.

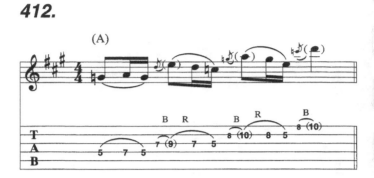

413.

414.

415.

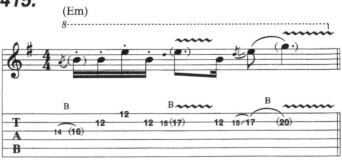

416.

417.

418.

419.

420.

421.

422.

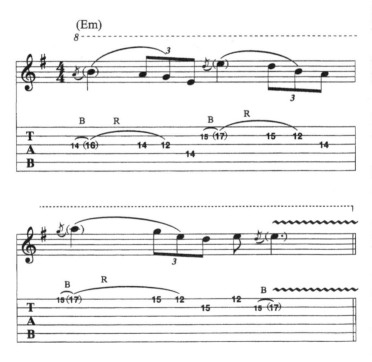

423.

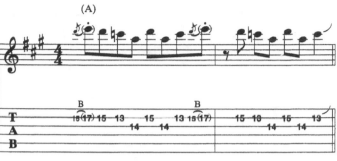

424.

425.

426.

427.

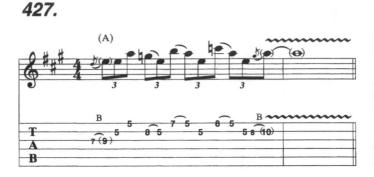

428.

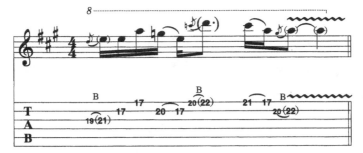

429.

430.

431.

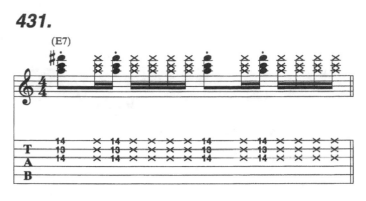

432.

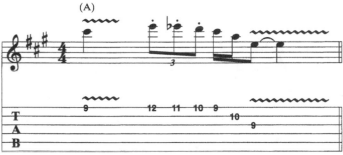

433.

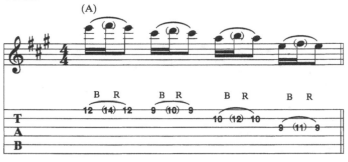

434.

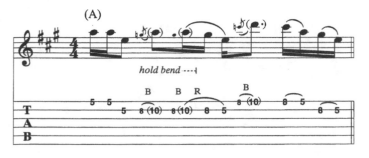

435.

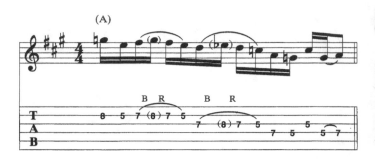

436.

437.

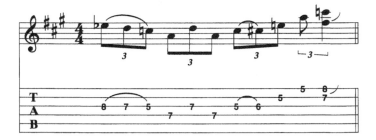

438.

439.

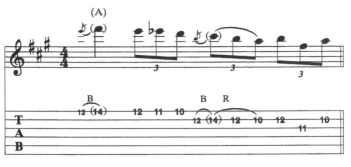

440.

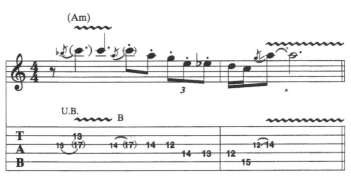

441.

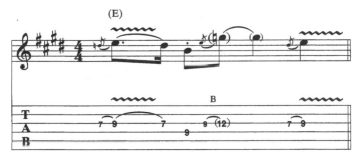

442.

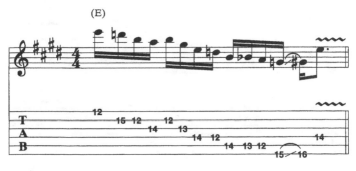

443.

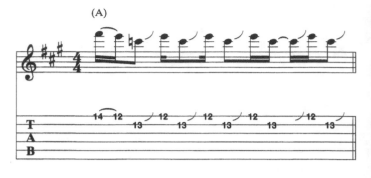

444.

445.

446.

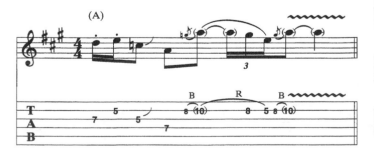

447.

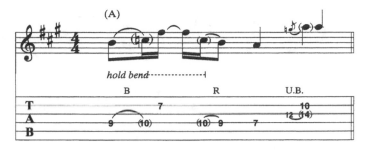

448.

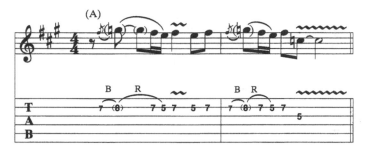

449.

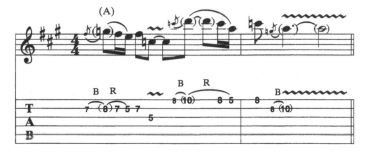

450.

451.

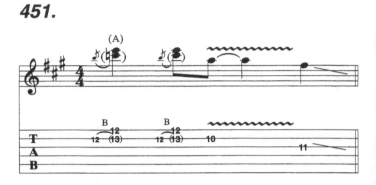

452.

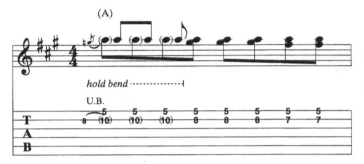

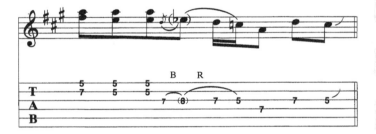

453.

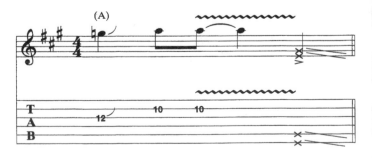

454.

455.

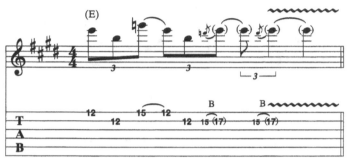

456.

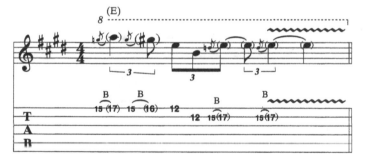

457.

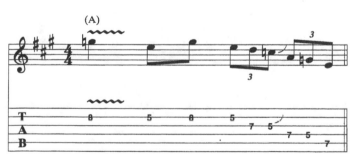

458.

459.

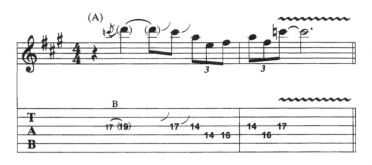

460.

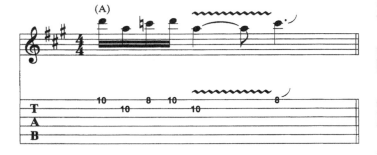

461.

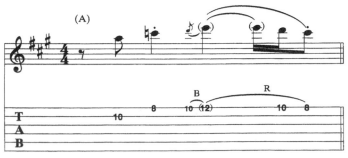

462.

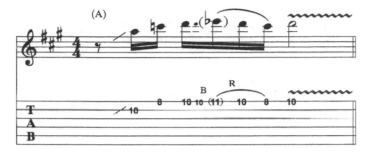

463.

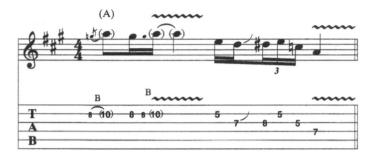

464.

465.

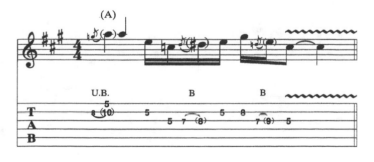

466.

467.

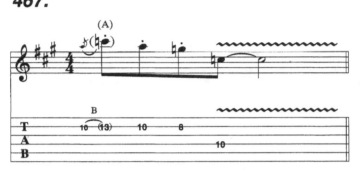

468.

469.

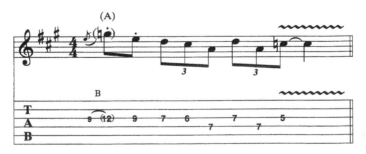

470.

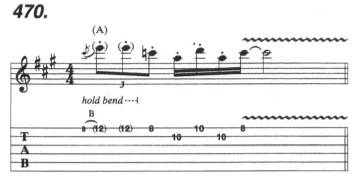

471.

472.

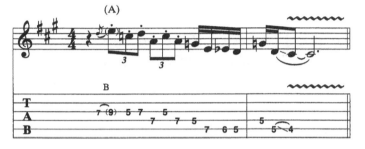

473.

474.

475.

476.

477.

478.

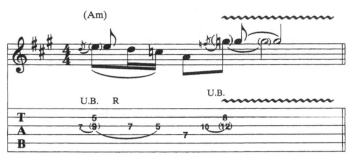

479.

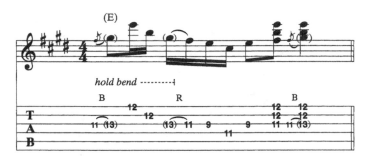

480.

481.

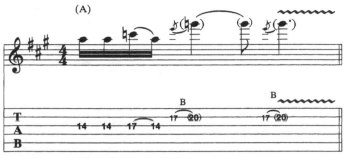

482.

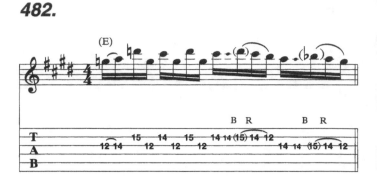

483.

484.

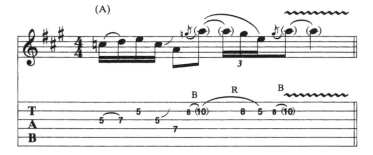

485.

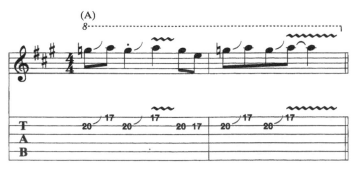

486.

487.

488.

489.

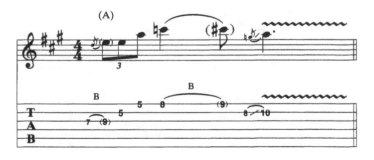

490.

491.

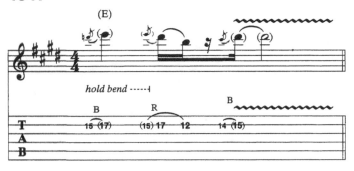

492.

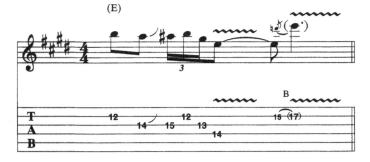

493.

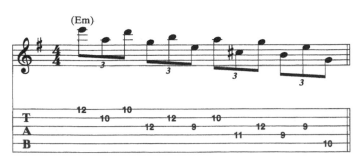

494.

495.

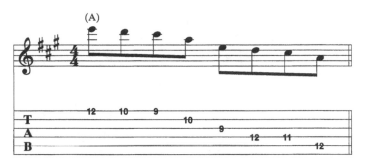

496.

497.

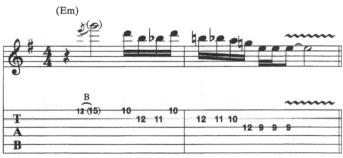

498.

499.

500.

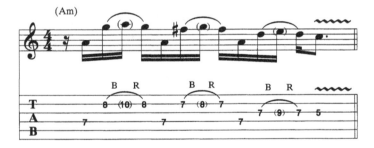

501.

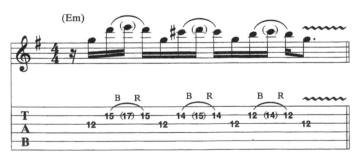

502.

503.

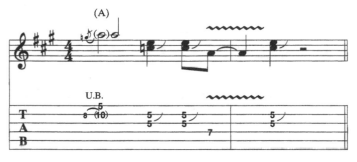

504.

505.

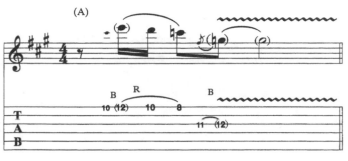

506.

507.

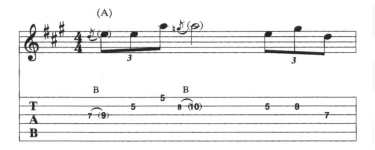

508.

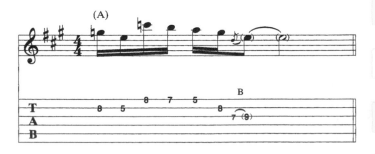

509.

510.

511.

512.

513.

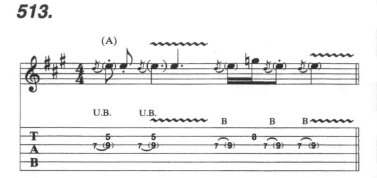

514.

515.

516.

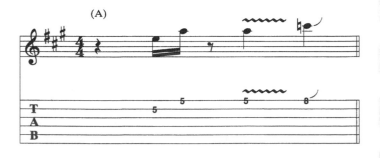

517.

518.

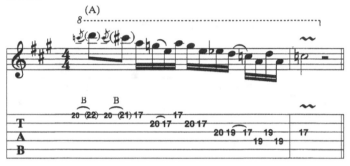

519.

520.

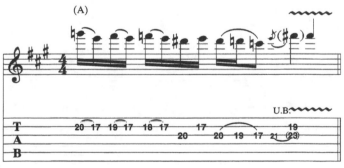

521.

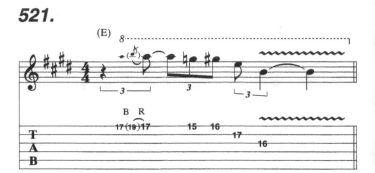

522.

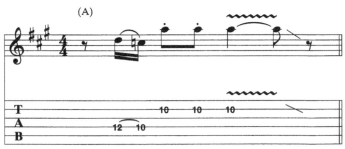

523.

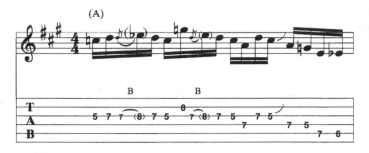

524.

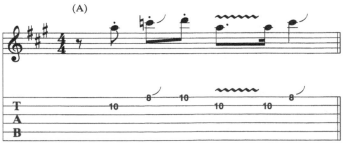

525.

526.

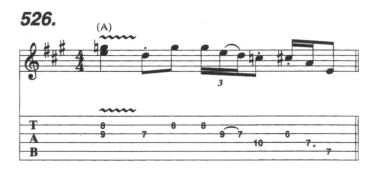

527.

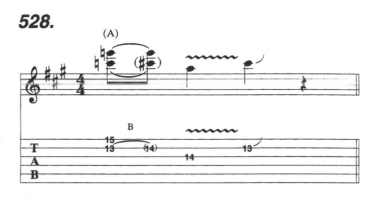

528.

529.

530.

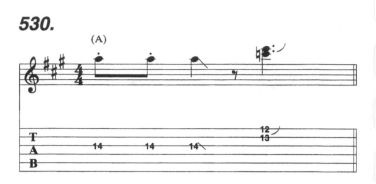

531.

532.

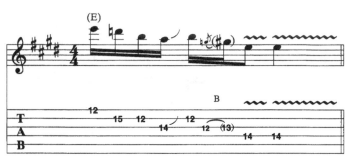

533.

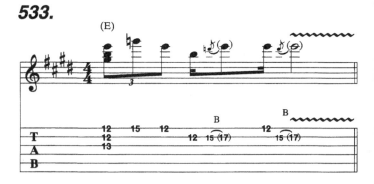

534.

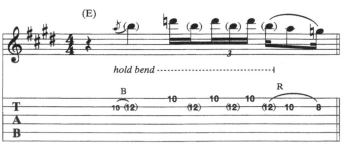

535.

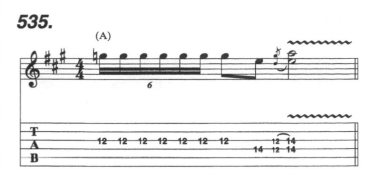

536.

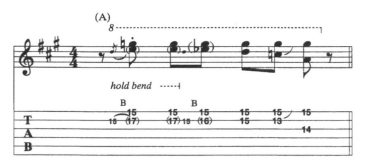

537.

538.

539.

540.

541.

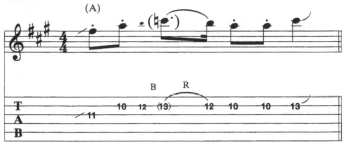

542.

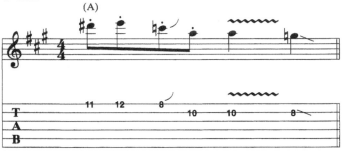

About the Author

Matt Scharfglass is a New York-based multi-instrumentalist, songwriter and guitar transcriber. As an instrumentalist, he can be frequently seen playing around New York City doing anything from gospel and musical theatre to chamber music and grunge. Recent session credits include spots for VH1.

With hundreds of transcriptions under his belt, Matt is a frequent contributor to *Guitar World;* his work can also be found in album folios published worldwide by companies such as Music Sales, Warner Brothers and Hal Leonard. Matt's other instructional books for Music Sales include *Beginning Blues Bass, First Step: Guitar for Kids,* and *Tuning Your Guitar.*

Matt is also the leader, guitarist and bassist of his own band, Mrs. Grundy, with two releases to its credit: *Your Stinky Candy* (1998), and *Booger* (2000), both on Screaming Yuppie Records and available at www.mrsgrundy.com. He likes to sneak up on his deaf cat and startle her in his spare time.